The Key Facts™ on

Mexico

Essential Information on Mexico

By Patrick W. Nee

The Internationalist®

www.internationalist.com

The Internationalist®

International Business, Investment, and Travel

Published by:

The Internationalist Publishing Company

96 Walter Street/ Suite 200

Boston, MA 02131, USA

Tel: 617-354-7722

www.internationalist.com

PN@internationalist.com

Table Of Contents

Chapter 1: Background

The site of several advanced Amerindian civilizations - including the Olmec, Toltec, Teotihuacan, Zapotec, Maya, and Aztec - Mexico was conquered and colonized by Spain in the early 16th century. Administered as the Viceroyalty of New Spain for three centuries, it achieved its independence early in the 19th century. The global financial crisis beginning in late 2008 caused a massive economic downturn the following year, although growth returned quickly in 2010. Ongoing economic and social concerns include low real wages, underemployment for a large segment of the population, inequitable income distribution, and few advancement opportunities for the largely indigenous population in the impoverished southern states. The elections held in 2000 marked the first time since the 1910 Mexican Revolution that an opposition candidate - Vicente FOX of the National Action Party (PAN) - defeated the party in government, the Institutional Revolutionary Party (PRI). He was succeeded in 2006 by another PAN candidate Felipe CALDERON, but the PRI regained the presidency in 2012. Since 2007, Mexico's powerful drug-trafficking organizations have engaged in bloody feuding, resulting in tens of thousands of drug-related homicides.

Chapter 2: Geography

Location:

North America, bordering the Caribbean Sea and the Gulf of Mexico, between Belize and the United States and bordering the North Pacific Ocean, between Guatemala and the United States

Geographic coordinates:

23 00 N, 102 00 W

Map references:

North America

Area:

total: 1,964,375 sq km

country comparison to the world: 14

land: 1,943,945 sq km

water: 20,430 sq km

Area - comparative:

slightly less than three times the size of Texas

Land boundaries:

total: 4,353 km

border countries: Belize 250 km, Guatemala 962 km, US 3,141 km

Coastline:

9,330 km

Maritime claims:

territorial sea: 12 nm

contiguous zone: 24 nm

exclusive economic zone: 200 nm

continental shelf: 200 nm or to the edge of the

continental margin

Climate:

varies from tropical to desert

Terrain:

high, rugged mountains; low coastal plains; high

plateaus; desert

Elevation extremes:

lowest point: Laguna Salada -10 m

highest point: Volcan Pico de Orizaba 5,700 m

Natural resources:

petroleum, silver, copper, gold, lead, zinc, natural gas,

timber

Land use:

arable land: 12.98%

permanent crops: 1.36%

other: 85.66% (2011)

Irrigated land:

64,600 sq km (2009)

Total renewable water resources:

457.2 cu km (2011)

**Freshwater withdrawal
(domestic/industrial/agricultural):**
> total: 80.4 cu km/yr (14%/9%/77%)
>
> per capita: 700.4 cu m/yr (2009)

Natural hazards:
> tsunamis along the Pacific coast, volcanoes and
> destructive earthquakes in the center and south, and
> hurricanes on the Pacific, Gulf of Mexico, and
> Caribbean coasts
>
> volcanism: volcanic activity in the central-southern
> part of the country; the volcanoes in Baja California
> are mostly dormant; Colima (elev. 3,850 m), which
> erupted in 2010, is Mexico's most active volcano and
> is responsible for causing periodic evacuations of
> nearby villagers; it has been deemed a "Decade
> Volcano" by the International Association of
> Volcanology and Chemistry of the Earth's Interior,
> worthy of study due to its explosive history and close
> proximity to human populations; Popocatepetl (elev.
> 5,426 m) poses a threat to Mexico City; other
> historically active volcanoes include Barcena,
> Ceboruco, El Chichon, Michoacan-Guanajuato, Pico
> de Orizaba, San Martin, Socorro, and Tacana

Environment - current issues:

scarcity of hazardous waste disposal facilities; rural to urban migration; natural freshwater resources scarce and polluted in north, inaccessible and poor quality in center and extreme southeast; raw sewage and industrial effluents polluting rivers in urban areas; deforestation; widespread erosion; desertification; deteriorating agricultural lands; serious air and water pollution in the national capital and urban centers along US-Mexico border; land subsidence in Valley of Mexico caused by groundwater depletion

note: the government considers the lack of clean water and deforestation national security issues

Environment - international agreements:

party to: Biodiversity, Climate Change, Climate Change-Kyoto Protocol, Desertification, Endangered Species, Hazardous Wastes, Law of the Sea, Marine Dumping, Marine Life Conservation, Ozone Layer Protection, Ship Pollution, Wetlands, Whaling

signed, but not ratified: none of the selected agreements

Geography - note:

strategic location on southern border of US; corn (maize), one of the world's major grain crops, is thought to have originated in Mexico

Chapter 3: People and Society

Nationality:

<u>noun</u>: Mexican(s)

<u>adjective</u>: Mexican

Ethnic groups:

mestizo (Amerindian-Spanish) 60%, Amerindian or predominantly Amerindian 30%, white 9%, other 1%

Languages:

Spanish only 92.7%, Spanish and indigenous languages 5.7%, indigenous only 0.8%, unspecified 0.8%

<u>note</u>: indigenous languages include various Mayan, Nahuatl, and other regional languages (2005)

Religions:

Roman Catholic 82.7%, Protestant 1.6%, Jehovah's Witnesses 1.4%, other Evangelical Churches 5%, other 1.9%, none 4.7%, unspecified 2.7% (2000 census)

Population:

116,220,947 (July 2013 est.)

<u>country comparison to the world</u>: 11

Age structure:

0-14 years: 27.4% (male 16,268,424/female 15,587,324)

15-24 years: 18.1% (male 10,566,890/female 10,421,798)

25-54 years: 40.7% (male 22,647,828/female 24,677,965)

55-64 years: 6.9% (male 3,703,316/female 4,337,956)

65 years and over: 6.9% (male 3,574,207/female 4,435,239) (2013 est.)

Median age:

total: 27.7 years

male: 26.6 years

female: 28.8 years (2013 est.)

Population growth rate:

1.07% (2013 est.)

country comparison to the world: 108

Birth rate:

18.61 births/1,000 population (2013 est.)

country comparison to the world: 103

Death rate:

4.94 deaths/1,000 population (2013 est.)

country comparison to the world: 187

Net migration rate:

-2.99 migrant(s)/1,000 population (2013 est.)

country comparison to the world: 176

Urbanization:

urban population: 78% of total population (2010)

rate of urbanization: 1.2% annual rate of change

(2010-15 est.)

note: Mexico City is the second-largest urban

agglomeration in the Western Hemisphere, after Sao

Paulo (Brazil), but before New York-Newark (US)

Major cities - population:

MEXICO CITY (capital) 19.319 million; Guadalajara

4.338 million; Monterrey 3.838 million; Puebla 2.278

million; Tijuana 1.629 million (2009)

Sex ratio:

at birth: 1.05 male(s)/female

0-14 years: 1.04 male(s)/female

15-24 years: 1.01 male(s)/female

25-54 years: 0.92 male(s)/female

55-64 years: 0.86 male(s)/female

65 years and over: 0.81 male(s)/female

total population: 0.96 male(s)/female (2013 est.)

Maternal mortality rate:

50 deaths/100,000 live births (2010)

country comparison to the world: 108

Infant mortality rate:

total: 16.26 deaths/1,000 live births

country comparison to the world: 103

male: 18.04 deaths/1,000 live births

female: 14.38 deaths/1,000 live births (2013 est.)

Life expectancy at birth:

total population: 76.86 years

country comparison to the world: 72

male: 74.03 years

female: 79.83 years (2013 est.)

Total fertility rate:

2.25 children born/woman (2013 est.)

country comparison to the world: 99

Health expenditures:

6.3% of GDP (2010)

country comparison to the world: 99

Physicians density:

2.89 physicians/1,000 population (2004)

Hospital bed density:

1.6 beds/1,000 population (2009)

Drinking water source:

improved:

urban: 97% of population

rural: 91% of population

total: 96% of population

unimproved:

    urban: 3% of population

    rural: 9% of population

    total: 4% of population (2010 est.)

Sanitation facility access:

improved:

    urban: 87% of population

    rural: 79% of population

    total: 85% of population

unimproved:

    urban: 13% of population

    rural: 21% of population

    total: 15% of population (2010 est.)

HIV/AIDS - adult prevalence rate:

0.3% (2009 est.)

country comparison to the world: 79

HIV/AIDS - people living with HIV/AIDS:

220,000 (2009 est.)

country comparison to the world: 25

HIV/AIDS - deaths:

NA

Major infectious diseases:

degree of risk: intermediate

<u>food or waterborne diseases</u>: bacterial diarrhea, hepatitis A, and typhoid fever

<u>vectorborne disease</u>: dengue fever

<u>water contact disease</u>: leptospirosis (2009)

Obesity - adult prevalence rate:

32.1% (2008)

<u>country comparison to the world</u>: 23

Children under the age of 5 years underweight:

3.4% (2006)

<u>country comparison to the world</u>: 103

Education expenditures:

5.3% of GDP (2009)

<u>country comparison to the world</u>: 63

Literacy:

<u>definition</u>: age 15 and over can read and write

<u>total population</u>: 86.1%

<u>male</u>: 86.9%

<u>female</u>: 85.3% (2005 Census)

School life expectancy (primary to tertiary education):

<u>total</u>: 14 years

<u>male</u>: 14 years

<u>female</u>: 14 years (2008)

Unemployment, youth ages 15-24:

<u>total</u>: 9.8%

<u>country comparison to the world</u>: 107

<u>male</u>: 9.5%

<u>female</u>: 10.4% (2011)

Chapter 4: Government and Key Leaders

Country name:

conventional long form: United Mexican States

conventional short form: Mexico

local long form: Estados Unidos Mexicanos

local short form: Mexico

Government type:

federal republic

Capital:

name: Mexico City (Distrito Federal)

geographic coordinates: 19 26 N, 99 08 W

time difference: UTC-6 (1 hour behind Washington,

DC during Standard Time)

daylight saving time: +1hr, begins first Sunday in

April; ends last Sunday in October

note: Mexico is divided into three time zones

Administrative divisions:

31 states (estados, singular - estado) and 1 federal

district* (distrito federal); Aguascalientes, Baja

California, Baja California Sur, Campeche, Chiapas,

Chihuahua, Coahuila de Zaragoza, Colima, Distrito

Federal*, Durango, Guanajuato, Guerrero, Hidalgo,

Jalisco, Mexico, Michoacan de Ocampo, Morelos,

Nayarit, Nuevo Leon, Oaxaca, Puebla, Queretaro de Arteaga, Quintana Roo, San Luis Potosi, Sinaloa, Sonora, Tabasco, Tamaulipas, Tlaxcala, Veracruz de Ignacio de la Llave (Veracruz), Yucatan, Zacatecas

Independence:

16 September 1810 (declared); 27 September 1821 (recognized by Spain)

National holiday:

Independence Day, 16 September (1810)

Constitution:

5 February 1917

Legal system:

civil law system with US constitutional law theory influence; judicial review of legislative acts

International law organization participation:

accepts compulsory ICJ jurisdiction with reservations; accepts ICCt jurisdiction

Suffrage:

18 years of age; universal and compulsory (but not enforced)

Executive branch:

chief of state: President Enrique PENA NIETO (since 1 December 2012); note - the president is both the chief of state and head of government

head of government: President Enrique PENA
NIETO (since 1 December 2012)

cabinet: Cabinet appointed by the president; note -
appointment of attorney general, the head of the Bank
of Mexico, and senior treasury officials require
consent of the Senate

elections: president elected by popular vote for a
single six-year term; election last held on 1 July 2012
(next to be held July 2018)

election results: Enrique PENA NIETO elected
president; percent of vote - Enrique PENA NIETO
(PRI) 38.21%, Andres Manuel LOPEZ OBRADOR
(PRD) 31.59%, Josefina Eugenia VAZQUEZ Mota
(PAN) 25.41%, other 4.79%

Legislative branch:

bicameral National Congress or Congreso de la Union
consists of the Senate or Camara de Senadores (128
seats; 96 members elected by popular vote to serve
six-year terms, and 32 seats allocated on the basis of
each party's popular vote) and the Chamber of
Deputies or Camara de Diputados (500 seats; 300
members are elected by popular vote; remaining 200
members are allocated on the basis of each party's
popular vote; members to serve three-year terms)

elections: Senate - last held on 1 July 2012 for all of the seats (next to be held on 1 July 2018); Chamber of Deputies - last held on 1 July 2012 (next to be held on 5 July 2015)

election results: Senate - percent of vote by party - NA; seats by party - PRI 52, PAN 38, PRD 22, PVEM 9, PT 4, Movimiento Ciudadano 2, PANAL 1; Chamber of Deputies - percent of vote by party - NA; seats by party - PRI 208, PAN 114, PRD 100, PVEM 33, PT 19, Movimiento Ciudadano 16, PANAL 10

Judicial branch:

Supreme Court of Justice or Suprema Corte de Justicia de la Nacion (justices or ministros are appointed by the president with consent of the Senate)

Political parties and leaders:

Citizen's Movement (Movimiento Ciudadano) [Luis WALTON Aburto]; Institutional Revolutionary Party (Partido Revolucionario Institucional) or PRI [Cesar CAMACHO Quiroz]; Labor Party (Partido del Trabajo) or PT [Alberto ANAYA Gutierrez]; Mexican Green Ecological Party (Partido Verde Ecologista de Mexico) or PVEM [vacant]; National Action Party (Partido Accion Nacional) or PAN [Gustavo MADERO Munoz]; New Alliance Party

(Partido Nueva Alianza) or PNA/PANAL [Luis CASTRO Obregon]; Party of the Democratic Revolution (Partido de la Revolucion Democratica) or PRD [Jesus ZAMBRANO Grijalva]

Political pressure groups and leaders:

Businessmen's Coordinating Council or CCE; Confederation of Employers of the Mexican Republic or COPARMEX; Confederation of Industrial Chambers or CONCAMIN; Confederation of Mexican Workers or CTM; Confederation of National Chambers of Commerce or CONCANACO; Coordinator for Foreign Trade Business Organizations or COECE; Federation of Unions Providing Goods and Services or FESEBES; National Chamber of Transformation Industries or CANACINTRA; National Peasant Confederation or CNC; National Small Business Chamber or CANACOPE; National Syndicate of Education Workers or SNTE; National Union of Workers or UNT; Popular Assembly of the People of Oaxaca or APPO; Roman Catholic Church

International organization participation:

APEC, BCIE, BIS, CAN (observer), Caricom (observer), CD, CDB, CE (observer), CELAC, CSN (observer), EBRD, FAO, FATF, G-20, G-3, G-15, G-24, IADB, IAEA, IBRD, ICAO, ICC (national committees), ICRM, IDA, IFAD, IFC, IFRCS, IHO, ILO, IMF, IMO, IMSO, Interpol, IOC, IOM, IPU, ISO, ITSO, ITU, ITUC (NGOs), LAES, LAIA, MIGA, NAFTA, NAM (observer), NEA, OAS, OECD, OPANAL, OPCW, Paris Club (associate), PCA, SICA (observer), UN, UNASUR (observer), UNCTAD, UNESCO, UNHCR, UNIDO, Union Latina (observer), UNWTO, UPU, WCO, WFTU (NGOs), WHO, WIPO, WMO, WTO

Diplomatic representation in the US:

chief of mission: Ambassador Eduardo MEDINA MORA Icaza

chancery: 1911 Pennsylvania Avenue NW, Washington, DC 20006

telephone: [1] (202) 728-1600

FAX: [1] (202) 728-1698

consulate(s) general: Anchorage, Atlanta, Austin, Boston, Chicago, Dallas, Denver, El Paso (TX), Houston, Laredo (TX), Los Angeles, Miami, New York, Nogales (AZ), Phoenix, Sacramento (CA), San Antonio, San Diego, San Francisco, San Jose (CA), San Juan (Puerto Rico), Saint Paul (MN) consulate(s): Albuquerque, Anchorage (AK), Boise (ID), Brownsville (TX), Calexico (CA), Del Rio (TX), Detroit, Douglas (AZ), Eagle Pass (TX), Fresno (CA), Indianapolis (IN), Kansas City (MO), Las Vegas (NV), Little Rock (AR), McAllen (TX), Midland (TX), New Orleans, Omaha (NE), Orlando (FL), Oxnard (CA), Philadelphia, Portland (OR), Presidio (TX), Raleigh (NC), Salt Lake City, San Bernardino (CA), Santa Ana (CA), Seattle, Tucson (AZ), Yuma (AZ); note - Washington DC Consular Section located in a separate building from the Mexican Embassy and has jurisdiction over DC, parts of Virginia, Maryland, and West Virginia

Diplomatic representation from the US:

chief of mission: Ambassador Earl Anthony WAYNE

embassy: Paseo de la Reforma 305, Colonia Cuauhtemoc, 06500 Mexico, Distrito Federal

mailing address: P. O. Box 9000, Brownsville, TX 78520-9000

telephone: [52] (55) 5080-2000

FAX: [52] (55) 5080-2834

consulate(s) general: Ciudad Juarez, Guadalajara, Hermosillo, Matamoros, Merida, Monterrey, Nogales, Nuevo Laredo, Tijuana

Key Leaders:

Pres.	Enrique PENA NIETO
Sec. of Agrarian Reform	Jorge Carlos RAMIREZ Marin
Sec. of Agriculture, Livestock, Rural Development, Fisheries, & Nutrition	Enrique MARTINEZ y Martinez
Sec. of Communications & Transport	Gerardo RUIZ Esparza
Sec. of Economy	Ildefonso GUAJARDO Villareal
Sec. of Energy	Pedro JOAQUIN COLDWELL
Sec. of Environment & Natural Resources	Juan Jose GUERRA Abud
Sec. of Finance & Public Credit	Luis VIDEGARAY Caso
Sec. of Foreign	Jose Antonio MEADE

Relations	Kuribrena
Sec. of Govt.	Miguel Angel OSORIO Chong
Sec. of Health	Mercedes Juan LOPEZ
Sec. of Labor & Social Welfare	Alfonso NAVARRETE Prida
Sec. of National Defense	Salvador CIENFUEGOS Zepeda,*Gen.*
Sec. of the Navy	Vidal SOBERON Sanz, *Adm.*
Sec. of Public Education	Emilio CHUAYFFET Chemor
Sec. of Public Security	
Sec. of Public Service	
Sec. of Social Development	Maria Del Rosario ROBLES Berlanga
Sec. of Tourism	Claudia RUIZ Massieu
Attorney Gen.	Jesus MURILLO Karam
Governor, Bank of Mexico	Agustin CARSTENS Carstens

Ambassador to the US	Eduardo MEDINA MORA Icaza
Permanent Representative to the UN, New York	Luis Alfonso DE ALBA Gongora

Flag description:

three equal vertical bands of green (hoist side), white, and red; Mexico's coat of arms (an eagle with a snake in its beak perched on a cactus) is centered in the white band; green signifies hope, joy, and love; white represents peace and honesty; red stands for hardiness, bravery, strength, and valor; the coat of arms is derived from a legend that the wandering Aztec people were to settle at a location where they would see an eagle on a cactus eating a snake; the city they founded, Tenochtitlan, is now Mexico City

note: similar to the flag of Italy, which is shorter, uses lighter shades of red and green, and does not have anything in its white band

National symbol(s):

golden eagle

National anthem:

<u>name</u>: "Himno Nacional Mexicano" (National Anthem of Mexico)

<u>lyrics/music</u>: Francisco Gonzalez BOCANEGRA/Jaime Nuno ROCA

<u>note</u>: adopted 1943, in use since 1854; the anthem is also known as "Mexicanos, al grito de Guerra" (Mexicans, to the War Cry); according to tradition, Francisco Gonzalez BOCANEGRA, an accomplished poet, was uninterested in submitting lyrics to a national anthem contest; his fiancee locked him in a room and refused to release him until the lyrics were completed

Chapter 5: Economy

Economy - overview:

Mexico has a free market economy in the trillion dollar class. It contains a mixture of modern and outmoded industry and agriculture, increasingly dominated by the private sector. Recent administrations have expanded competition in seaports, railroads, telecommunications, electricity generation, natural gas distribution, and airports. Per capita income is roughly one-third that of the US; income distribution remains highly unequal. Since the implementation of the North American Free Trade Agreement (NAFTA) in 1994, Mexico's share of US imports has increased from 7% to 12%, and its share of Canadian imports has doubled to 5.5%. Mexico has free trade agreements with over 50 countries including Guatemala, Honduras, El Salvador, the European Free Trade Area, and Japan - putting more than 90% of trade under free trade agreements. In 2012 Mexico formally joined the Trans-Pacific Partnership negotiations and in July it formed the Pacific Alliance with Peru, Colombia and Chile. In 2007, during its first year in office, the Felipe

CALDERON administration was able to garner support from the opposition to successfully pass pension and fiscal reforms. The administration passed an energy reform measure in 2008 and another fiscal reform in 2009. Mexico's GDP plunged 6.2% in 2009 as world demand for exports dropped, asset prices tumbled, and remittances and investment declined. GDP posted positive growth of 5.6% in 2010 with exports - particularly to the United States - leading the way. Growth slowed to 3.9% in 2011 and slightly recovered to 4% in 2012. In November 2012, Mexico's legislature passed a comprehensive labor reform which was signed into law by former President Felipe CALDERON. Mexico's new PRI government, led by President Enrique PENA NIETO, has said it will prioritize structural economic reforms and competitiveness. The new president signed the Pact for Mexico, an agreement that lists 95 priority commitments, along with the leaders of the country's three main political parties: the Institutional Revolutionary Party (PRI), the National Action Party (PAN) and the Party of the Democratic Revolution (PRD).

GDP (purchasing power parity):

$1.761 trillion (2012 est.)

country comparison to the world: 12

$1.694 trillion (2011 est.)

$1.629 trillion (2010 est.)

note: data are in 2012 US dollars

GDP (official exchange rate):

$1.163 trillion (2012 est.)

GDP - real growth rate:

4% (2012 est.)

country comparison to the world: 85

3.9% (2011 est.)

5.6% (2010 est.)

GDP - per capita (PPP):

$15,300 (2012 est.)

country comparison to the world: 88

$14,900 (2011 est.)

$14,500 (2010 est.)

note: data are in 2012 US dollars

GDP - composition by sector:

agriculture: 3.7%

industry: 34.2%

services: 62.1% (2012 est.)

Labor force:

50.7 million (2012 est.)

country comparison to the world: 12
Labor force - by occupation:

agriculture: 13.7%

industry: 23.4%

services: 62.9% (2005)

Unemployment rate:

5% (2012 est.)

country comparison to the world: 47

5.2% (2011 est.)

note: underemployment may be as high as 25%

Population below poverty line:

51.3%

note: based on food-based definition of poverty; asset based poverty amounted to more than 47% (2010 est.)

Household income or consumption by percentage share:

lowest 10%: 1.5%

highest 10%: 41.4% (2008)

Distribution of family income - Gini index:

48.3 (2008)

country comparison to the world: 25

53.1 (1998)

Investment (gross fixed):

21.5% of GDP (2012 est.)

country comparison to the world: 77

Budget:

revenues: $276.2 billion

expenditures: $308.2 billion (2012 est.)

Taxes and other revenues:

23.8% of GDP (2012 est.)

country comparison to the world: 131

Budget surplus (+) or deficit (-):

-2.8% of GDP (2012 est.)

country comparison to the world: 103

Public debt:

35.4% of GDP (2012 est.)

country comparison to the world: 101

35.4% of GDP (2011 est.)

Inflation rate (consumer prices):

3.6% (2012 est.)

country comparison to the world: 101

3.4% (2011 est.)

Central bank discount rate:

NA%

4.5% (31 December 2012 est.)

country comparison to the world: 80

4.5% (31 December 2011 est.)

Commercial bank prime lending rate:

4.7% (31 December 2012 est.)

country comparison to the world: 159

4.92% (31 December 2011 est.)

Stock of narrow money:

$180.7 billion (31 December 2012 est.)

country comparison to the world: 20

$148.9 billion (31 December 2011 est.)

Stock of broad money:

$738 billion (31 December 2012 est.)

country comparison to the world: 20

$684.1 billion (31 December 2011 est.)

Stock of domestic credit:

$445.6 billion (31 December 2012 est.)

country comparison to the world: 27

$359.5 billion (31 December 2011 est.)

Market value of publicly traded shares:

$408.7 billion (31 December 2011)

country comparison to the world: 22

$454.3 billion (31 December 2010)

$340.6 billion (31 December 2009)

Agriculture - products:

corn, wheat, soybeans, rice, beans, cotton, coffee, fruit, tomatoes; beef, poultry, dairy products; wood products

Industries:

food and beverages, tobacco, chemicals, iron and steel, petroleum, mining, textiles, clothing, motor vehicles, consumer durables, tourism

Industrial production growth rate:

3.6% (2012 est.)

country comparison to the world: 78

Current account balance:

$-11 billion (2012 est.)

country comparison to the world: 176

$-11.07 billion (2011 est.)

Exports:

$370.9 billion (2012 est.)

country comparison to the world: 16

$349.4 billion (2011 est.)

Exports - commodities:

manufactured goods, oil and oil products, silver, fruits, vegetables, coffee, cotton

Exports - partners:

US 78% (2012)

Imports:

$379.4 billion (2012 est.)

country comparison to the world: 15

$350.8 billion (2011 est.)

Imports - commodities:

metalworking machines, steel mill products, agricultural machinery, electrical equipment, car parts for assembly, repair parts for motor vehicles, aircraft, and aircraft parts

Imports - partners:

US 49.7%, China 14.9%, Japan 4.7% (2011)

Reserves of foreign exchange and gold:

$163.6 billion (31 December 2012 est.)

country comparison to the world: 18

$149.3 billion (31 December 2011 est.)

Debt - external:

$125.7 billion (31 December 2012 est.)

country comparison to the world: 40

$210.9 billion (31 December 2011 est.)

Stock of direct foreign investment - at home:

$301.9 billion (31 December 2012 est.)

country comparison to the world: 18

$288.9 billion (31 December 2011 est.)

Stock of direct foreign investment - abroad:

$129.7 billion (31 December 2012 est.)

country comparison to the world: 26

$112.1 billion (31 December 2011 est.)

Exchange rates:

Mexican pesos (MXN) per US dollar -

13.25 (2012 est.)

12.42 (2011 est.)

12.64 (2010 est.)

13.51 (2009)

11.02 (2008)

Fiscal year:

calendar year

Chapter 6: Energy

Electricity - production:

254.4 billion kWh (2010 est.)

country comparison to the world: 17

Electricity - consumption:

203.8 billion kWh (2009 est.)

country comparison to the world: 19

Electricity - exports:

1.32 billion kWh (2010 est.)

country comparison to the world: 50

Electricity - imports:

624.5 million kWh (2010 est.)

country comparison to the world: 71

Electricity - installed generating capacity:

59.33 million kW (2009 est.)

country comparison to the world: 15

Electricity - from fossil fuels:

75% of total installed capacity (2009 est.)

country comparison to the world: 101

Electricity - from nuclear fuels:

2.3% of total installed capacity (2009 est.)

country comparison to the world: 28

Electricity - from hydroelectric plants:

19.4% of total installed capacity (2009 est.)

country comparison to the world: 92

Electricity - from other renewable sources:

3.3% of total installed capacity (2009 est.)

country comparison to the world: 45

Crude oil - production:

2.934 million bbl/day (2011 est.)

country comparison to the world: 9

Crude oil - exports:

1.299 million bbl/day (2009 est.)

country comparison to the world: 13

Crude oil - imports:

0 bbl/day (2009 est.)

country comparison to the world: 102

Crude oil - proved reserves:

12.17 billion bbl (1 January 2013 es)

country comparison to the world: 19

Refined petroleum products - production:

1.458 million bbl/day (2009 est.)

country comparison to the world: 17

Refined petroleum products - consumption:

2.133 million bbl/day (2011 est.)

country comparison to the world: 13

Refined petroleum products - exports:

199,000 bbl/day (2009 est.)

country comparison to the world: 33

Refined petroleum products - imports:

496,000 bbl/day (2009 est.)

country comparison to the world: 12

Natural gas - production:

55.1 billion cu m (2011 est.)

country comparison to the world: 18

Natural gas - consumption:

59.15 billion cu m (2011 est.)

country comparison to the world: 15

Natural gas - exports:

13 million cu m (2011 est.)

country comparison to the world: 49

Natural gas - imports:

13.95 billion cu m (2011 est.)

country comparison to the world: 22

Natural gas - proved reserves:

490.3 billion cu m (1 January 2012 es)

country comparison to the world: 32

Carbon dioxide emissions from consumption of energy:

445.3 million Mt (2010 est.)

country comparison to the world: 15

Chapter 7: Communications

Telephones - main lines in use:

19.684 million (2011)

country comparison to the world: 15

Telephones - mobile cellular:

94.565 million (2011)

country comparison to the world: 13

Telephone system:

general assessment: adequate telephone service for business and government; improving quality and increasing mobile cellular availability, with mobile subscribers far outnumbering fixed-line subscribers; domestic satellite system with 120 earth stations; extensive microwave radio relay network; considerable use of fiber-optic cable and coaxial cable

domestic: despite the opening to competition in January 1997, Telmex remains dominant; Fixed-line teledensity is less than 20 per 100 persons; mobile-cellular teledensity is about 80 per 100 persons

international: country code - 52; Columbus-2 fiber-optic submarine cable with access to the US, Virgin Islands, Canary Islands, Spain, and Italy; the

Americas Region Caribbean Ring System (ARCOS-1) and the MAYA-1 submarine cable system together provide access to Central America, parts of South America and the Caribbean, and the US; satellite earth stations - 120 (32 Intelsat, 2 Solidaridad (giving Mexico improved access to South America, Central America, and much of the US as well as enhancing domestic communications), 1 Panamsat, numerous Inmarsat mobile earth stations); linked to Central American Microwave System of trunk connections (2011)

Broadcast media:

many TV stations and more than 1,400 radio stations with most privately owned; the Televisa group once had a virtual monopoly in TV broadcasting, but new broadcasting groups and foreign satellite and cable operators are now available (2012)

Internet country code:

.mx

Internet hosts:

16.233 million (2012)

country comparison to the world: 9

Internet users:

31.02 million (2009)

country comparison to the world: 12

Chapter 8: Transportation

Airports:

    1,724 (2012)

    country comparison to the world: 3

Airports - with paved runways:

    total: 249

    over 3,047 m: 12

    2,438 to 3,047 m: 30

    1,524 to 2,437 m: 82

    914 to 1,523 m: 88

    under 914 m: 37 (2012)

Airports - with unpaved runways:

    total: 1,475

    over 3,047 m: 1

    2,438 to 3,047 m: 2

    1,524 to 2,437 m: 44

    914 to 1,523 m: 288

    under 914 m: 1,140 (2012)

Heliports:

    1 (2012)

Pipelines:

gas 16,594 km; liquid petroleum gas 2,152 km; oil 7,499 km; oil/gas/water 4 km; refined products 7,264 km; water 33 km (2010)

Railways:

total: 17,166 km

country comparison to the world: 16

standard gauge: 17,166 km 1.435-m gauge (22 km electrified) (2008)

Roadways:

total: 366,095 km

country comparison to the world: 17

paved: 132,289 km (includes 6,279 km of expressways)

unpaved: 233,806 km (2008)

Waterways:

2,900 km (navigable rivers and coastal canals mostly connected with ports on the country's east coast) (2012)

country comparison to the world: 34

Merchant marine:

total: 52

country comparison to the world: 70

by type: bulk carrier 5, cargo 3, chemical tanker 11, liquefied gas 3, passenger/cargo 10, petroleum tanker 17, roll on/roll off 3

foreign-owned: 5 (France 1, Greece 2, South Africa 1, UAE 1)

registered in other countries: 12 (Antigua and Barbuda 1, Marshall Islands 2, Panama 5, Portugal 1, Spain 1, Venezuela 1, unknown 1) (2010)

Ports and terminals:

Altamira, Coatzacoalcos, Lazaro Cardenas, Manzanillo, Salina Cruz, Veracruz

oil terminals: Cayo Arcas terminal, Dos Bocas terminal

Chapter 9: Military

Military branches:

Secretariat of National Defense (Secretaria de Defensa Nacional, Sedena): Army (Ejercito), Mexican Air Force (Fuerza Aerea Mexicana, FAM); Secretariat of the Navy (Secretaria de Marina, Semar): Mexican Navy (Armada de Mexico (ARM), includes Naval Air Force (FAN), Mexican Marine Corps (Cuerpo de Infanteria de Marina, Mexmar or CIM)) (2011)

Military service age and obligation:

18 years of age for compulsory military service, conscript service obligation - 12 months; 16 years of age with consent for voluntary enlistment; conscripts serve only in the Army; Navy and Air Force service is all voluntary; women are eligible for voluntary military service (2007)

Manpower available for military service:

males age 16-49: 28,815,506

females age 16-49: 30,363,558 (2010 est.)

Manpower fit for military service:

males age 16-49: 23,239,866

females age 16-49: 25,642,549 (2010 est.)

Manpower reaching militarily significant age annually:

male: 1,105,371

female: 1,067,007 (2010 est.)

Military expenditures:

0.5% of GDP (2012)

country comparison to the world: 161

Chapter 10: Transnational Issues

Disputes - international:

abundant rainfall in recent years along much of the Mexico-US border region has ameliorated periodically strained water-sharing arrangements; the US has intensified security measures to monitor and control legal and illegal personnel, transport, and commodities across its border with Mexico; Mexico must deal with thousands of impoverished Guatemalans and other Central Americans who cross the porous border looking for work in Mexico and the United States; Belize and Mexico are working to solve minor border demarcation discrepancies arising from inaccuracies in the 1898 border treaty

Refugees and internally displaced persons:

IDPs: 160,000 (government's quashing of Zapatista uprising in 1994 in eastern Chiapas Region; drug cartel violence and government's military response since 2007; violence between and within indigenous groups) (2011)

Illicit drugs:

major drug-producing and transit nation; world's second largest opium poppy cultivator; opium poppy cultivation in 2009 rose 31% over 2008 to 19,500 hectares yielding a potential production of 50 metric tons of pure heroin, or 125 metric tons of "black tar" heroin, the dominant form of Mexican heroin in the western United States; marijuana cultivation increased 45% to 17,500 hectares in 2009; government conducts the largest independent illicit-crop eradication program in the world; continues as the primary transshipment country for US-bound cocaine from South America, with an estimated 95% of annual cocaine movements toward the US stopping in Mexico; major drug syndicates control the majority of drug trafficking throughout the country; producer and distributor of ecstasy; significant money-laundering center; major supplier of heroin and largest foreign supplier of marijuana and methamphetamine to the US market (2007)

Map of Mexico

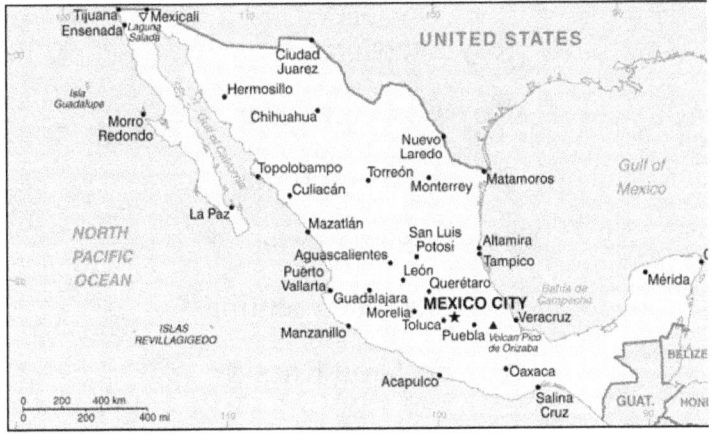

Other Key Facts™ Titles

Key Facts on South Korea

Key Facts on France

Key Facts on the United Kingdom

Key Facts on Egypt

Key Facts on Israel

All Key Facts™ Titles are Available at

www.Amazon.com

THE INTERNATIONALIST®

2013

WWW.INTERNATIONALIST.COM